The Power of Silence

Winning The Battle Over The Noise Of Life (Inner Life, Introversion, Busy Life, Power Of Quiet, Slowing Down)

Lance P. Richards

The Power of Silence: Winning The Battle Over The Noise Of Life (Inner Life, Introversion, Busy Life, Power Of Quiet, Slowing Down)

This book was self-published with the amazing help of Self-Publishing Made Easy Now! [1] . You can grab a free copy of the checklist that started my journey here: FREE Self-Publishing Checklist [2] .

[1] https://selfpublishingmadeeasynow.com/xpjv
[2] https://selfpublishingmadeeasynow.com/free_checklist

Table of Contents

1 - Introduction

Do you constantly find yourself stressed out, tired, or overwhelmed? Do you want to step away from the noise of life? Are you looking for simple yet effective strategies to attain rest and relaxation?

If so, then this book definitely has what you are looking for!

This book will share with you the reasons why silence can be the most effective way towards attaining peace of mind and clarity of thought. More importantly, you will find here the strategies that will let you make the most of these quiet times of solitude.

You can also expect to find practical solutions on how to understand your inner self, create your quiet space, and simplify your daily life. Aside from these, you will also learn how to develop habits that you can thoroughly enjoy in the midst of peaceful and silent solitude, including a digital detox, journaling, meditating, connecting with nature, and reading for pleasure.

This book is dedicated to those who want to break free from the daily grind, those who wish to discover the more hidden aspects of themselves, and those who simply want to appreciate life in the present moment.

Begin your journey towards discovering the power of silence now. So, without further ado, onto chapter 2.

2 - The Power of Silence

"True silence is the rest of the mind, and is to the spirit what sleep is to the body, nourishment, and refreshment."

William Penn

The modern world has become filled with so much more stimuli than it ever did before, especially now with all the latest advancements. Every which way we turn, there always seems to be something going on that we often times could not help but try to become a part of it.

For instance, we have instant chat messaging to communicate with everyone from our next-door neighbor to our friends from across the globe, when back then we had to wait for weeks before receiving a reply. Libraries might not even be as popular nowadays because we can now save thousands of books and other sources of information within a palm-sized device.

Back then, people also had to visit the public library and scour through shelves upon shelves to find the reference they are looking for. Now, it takes a few seconds for anyone to find answers to most of their questions because of search engines like Google.

Of course, we must be thankful for all of these amazing inventions because they have made life much more convenient, to say the least. They have helped a lot of people broaden their knowledge and skills, got people together into one platform without leaving their homes so as to discuss and collaborate on innovations, and they have millions of ways to entertain us and help us escape from the humdrum of routine.

The problem only starts when we become so wrapped up in the activity and noise of our world that we fail to appreciate the other aspect of our lives: silence.

When people talk about silence, they usually refer to the absence of sound. Silence is a word most people usually associate with libraries and other really "strict" institutions because it discourages people from talking to each other and being a disturbance.

Silence is also a way of protesting, of refusing to speak even when expected to. When we are angry or disappointed, silence is sometimes the preferred way to show how we feel without really saying anything.

As you can see, silence has many meanings. In this book, however, it refers to freedom from noise and agitation, from disturbances, stress, and intense emotions.

To be in a place of quiet means to be in a place where much input – the opinions of other people, auditory experiences such as music blasting from one's earphones, the pressures of the workplace – cannot penetrate into your mind. It is a time when you have enough energy and space to enter into a deep state of thought.

To inspire you to have more moments of stillness, peace and quiet, here are some of the benefits you can gain from the power of silence:

It is good for our mind.

Our everyday lives are now bombarded with so much sensory input that the World Health Organization has even referred to it as a "modern plague" that negatively affects one's health. Indeed, many of us have become so used to always listening to music, watching videos online, and practically overloading our senses with stimuli, that we are inadvertently triggering unnecessary stress and tension.

Moments of silence, on the other hand, can help the brain the brain restore itself. It fact, silence may be more effective at stabilizing blood circulation than relaxing sounds, according to a study published in the April 2006 issue of the journal Heart.

Another study, published in the December 2013 issue of Brain Structure and Function, reveals that silence can help the brain regenerate new cells in its hippocampus or the region linked to our memory, emotions, and ability to learn.

It helps us tap our inner self.

Our inner self can be defined in many terms, depending on what their motive is, but in this particular book, it simply refers to the stream of ideas, thoughts, emotions, and memories that flow in your mind and that you can witness and understand better without the distractions of the outside world. The only way to really engage with our inner self is by eliminating distractions and entering the state of silence.

The advantages to tapping our inner self are plentiful. For one, it helps you unleash your creativity. People widely known for their intelligence and creativity such as Albert Einstein, Alexander Graham Bell, Lewis Carroll, and T.S. Eliot, have praised the effects of solitude and silence on their thinking process, and they give it part of the credit for what they have created.

It brings to light our unhealthy habits.

Have there been times when you swear to quit a bad habit, only to find yourself being hooked to it more than ever? Or maybe you believe yourself to be stuck in an unhealthy relationship with someone, but it is somehow challenging for you to stop communicating with that person or making excuses for their behavior.

Whatever your unhealthy habits may be, you can only recognize them for what they truly are and how much damage they have caused in your life if you spend some time in silent thought.

The beauty in this, though, is that you will also be able to see the most effective means by which you can overcome these unhealthy habits. Naturally, it won't make the transition easier, but you will be able to solve your problems better.

It helps us put things into perspective.

Picture a fresh graduate who wants to start her own company and has decided to work for a company from which she wants to learn the ropes and earn enough for her start-up capital at the same time.

Along the way, she encounters so much gossip, idea stealing, and "politicking" among her peers and so many crazy demands and fits of anger from her boss that she decides to put in less effort, clock in fewer hours, and even join in on the power play. In the process, she began to lose sight of what she originally aspired for − the dream business she had been dreaming of right when she graduated from college.

You have probably experienced many hiccups in the daily grind yourself, and it might have caused you to let go of certain aspirations in your life. Indeed, there are times when we feel so overcome by difficulties that we would go so far as to contemplate quitting.

However, if we try to disengage from the throes caused by failure and tribulations and through silence consider our reasons behind the struggle, we will be able to rekindle our passion towards the goal we wish to achieve.

It reminds us of what is important.

Have you ever encountered a little exercise wherein you are asked to imagine yourself in your own wake, surrounded by the people whom you believe would visit you at your funeral? If you have not, then you might like to give it a try. If you have, then it would still be a good idea to try it again as a gentle reminder. Here is how you can do it:

Find a cool, quiet and dim place where you can lie down undisturbed for a few minutes. Once you are there, go ahead and lie down comfortably. Close your eyes. Now, imagine that you are in a wake, your wake. All the people you know have been informed of your passing.

In your mind's eye, visualize who the people in your wake are. Can you find the ones who matter the most to you? How are they coping with you being gone? Lay silently as you imagine each person and what they would say about you, or even what they are thinking as they gaze at your lifeless body.

Now, spend some time looking back on how you lived your life up until today. Would you say you had lived it free from regrets? If you do have some regrets, what are they and why do you regret them

consider them to regret? If you still had the opportunity to go back and fix them, would you? How would you go about it?

Try not to rush through this experience, because you would

be able to commune with your mind in such a way that it cannot be replicated in any other situation. Allow your thoughts to flow freely, and if a particular thought stirs up your emotions, let yourself express these feelings as well.

This is the beauty of silence, as it allows you to call forth your deep-seated thoughts and then, hopefully, spark you to pursue the things that you might regret if you had not.

Naturally, you would be able to have more unique experiences and enjoy personal benefits from the power of silence. Of course, the only way to find out what these could be is to practice having moments of quiet every day.

The rest of this book will give you plenty of tips and ideas on how, through silence, you can learn more about your thoughts, emotions and unleash your mind's full potential, and win the battle against the noise of life.

3 - Understanding your Inner Self

"There is an amazing power getting to know your inner self and learning how to use it and not fight with the world. If you know what makes you happy, your personality, interests, and capabilities, just use them, and everything else flows beautifully."

Juhi Chawla

Are you an Introvert or Extrovert?

Do you like to read books or articles about psychology or personality types? Those who do are most likely familiar with the concepts of introversion and extroversion. However, if you are unsure of whether you are an introvert or extrovert, you can try answering the following questions with a yes or no:

- You have been told you are a good listener.

- You are fond of writing your thoughts out on paper more than you do talking about them to a friend.

- You tend to spend more time conversing with just one person than with a group of people.

- You like spending time alone.

- You prefer to discuss deeply about topics that are important to you than to make small talk.

- You do not like getting into arguments with other people so you prefer to keep quiet when you are upset.

- You like doing work yourself than collaborating with others.

- You have been described as quiet or soft-spoken for more than once in your life.

- Your idea of a happy celebration is experiencing it with close family and/or friends instead of a large group.

- You do not find it difficult to focus on a task for an extended period of time.

- When someone calls you, you sometimes tend to let it go through to voice mail or consider not answering and then just texting them afterwards.

- After a day out in public such as when you go shopping, you come home feeling tired even if you did enjoy the activity.

- You like to take your time thinking about how to respond to something before you say your thoughts aloud.

- You are disinclined to share your opinions, achievements, and/or life's moments on social media.

- You would rather not discuss or reveal your work to your peers until you have completed it.

So, now that you have answered all of these statements, count how many times you said "yes." If out of 15 statements at least 10 of your answers are yes, then you are more of an introvert.

The reverse is true if at least 10 are no. If your answers are a roughly equal distribution of yes and no, then you may be able to call yourself an ambivert – or someone who is inclined to be introverted in an equal number of situations as he/she is extroverted.

Some people think introverts are the shy ones and extroverts are the loud ones, but that is actually not the way it works. Rather, you can tell whether you are an introvert or an extrovert based on how you restore your energy.

On one end of the spectrum, extroverts feel happier, stronger, and more energized when they spend time with other people, which means they tend to lose energy when they are alone.

Introverts are the exact opposite, in that they gain energy and happiness when they are in solitude, and their energy is depleted when they socialize, especially with large groups of people.

Take note that introversion should not be mistaken for shyness, or the fear of being embarrassed because there are plenty of confident introverts who do not hesitate to engage in an animated conversation with strangers if it is a topic that means a lot to them.

Also, some extroverts happen to be shy, and this proves to be a difficult situation for them because, despite their constant need for companionship, their shyness keeps them from approaching others.

The reason why it is so important for people to know whether they is an introvert or an extrovert is so they can understand why they feel or act in a certain way during specific situations. For instance, introverts who are unaware of their nature could suffer in silence for years in a society biased towards extroverts.

Do you currently have a Fixed or Growth Mindset?

Have you ever heard of the concept "fixed and growth mindset?" It was discovered by a psychology professor named Carol S. Dweck, who discussed this in detail in her 2006 book Mindset: The New Psychology of Success. But before we talk about that, you can answer the following questions to determine whether the way your mindset works right now is leaning towards the fixed or the growth kind.

It is best to have a pen and paper ready. To answer these statements, write 4 for "completely agree," 3 for "agree," 2 D "disagree," and 1 for "completely disagree."

- I am at a certain level of intelligence that I cannot really do much about.

- My intelligence is who I am.

- Not everyone can become smart no matter how hard they try.

- Each of us is born with a set of talents.

- It is always stressful when you are trying out new things.

- Some people are born kind, and some are born cruel. That's how the world works.

- Feedback from other people is hard to accept.

- Smart people do not have to try as hard as the not so smart ones to get good grades at school.

- It is important to look smart all the time so people will respect you.

- You think it is hard to lose weight and not everyone is capable of doing it.

After that, you have given your answer to these statements. You can go ahead and total your score. If your score is between 31 and 40, then you are likely to have a fixed mindset right now.

If it is between 21 and 30 then it means most of your ideas could be fixed, but not all. If you got between 11 and 20 then you probably have an equal number of fixed and growth mindset-based ideas. But if it is 10, then you are likely to have a growth mindset.

Now, take note that this test should never define who you are because there are not enough statements and scenarios to really help you dig deeper into your inner self, as far as your mindset goes. However, it does serve as a "peek" into the way your mindset works. That said, let us now talk about the difference between a "fixed" versus a "growth" mindset.

Carol Dweck describes the fixed and growth mindsets in relation to learners. She said that learners or students who have a fixed mindset are those who think that their intelligence, talents, and abilities are fixed traits.

Specifically, they believe they have a certain amount of these traits and that there is nothing they could do about it. Also, the goal of those who have a fixed mindset is to always look smart to others and to avoid looking stupid.

On the other side of the spectrum are the learners with a growth mindset, who believe that they can develop their intelligence, talents, and abilities as long as they put in the effort, are persistent, and have good teachers. While most of them do not think everyone can become like "Einstein," they do think they can "get smarter" as long as they try hard enough.

In a nutshell, those with the fixed mindset believe everything is set or fixed. Those with the growth mindset, on the other hand, believe they can continue to grow if they so try. It is so important for anyone to know which of the two mindsets their inner self is feeding because then they would be able to do something about it.

In fact, by believing that you can do something about, you are already starting to think in the growth mindset way. With the help of introspection and the power of silence, you can take the time to listen to how your inner self-perceives itself and the world as well as responds to situations.

Developing the growth mindset and diminishing fixed ideas will enable you to achieve anything you want. It will dramatically boost your self-confidence and also help you become more optimistic towards your goals and abilities.

You will also be able to help other people who are still struggling with a fixed mindset because then you could explain to them that they can be smarter, more creative, stronger, faster, more intelligent, and successful if they focus on improving themselves constantly.

What are your Values in Life?

Your values are basically your beliefs in which you are emotionally invested, which means you hold them with utmost importance. Whatever we encounter that is not in line with our values, we reject. However, if we are thrust into a situation in which we cannot say no to whatever is not in line with them, then our lives would become miserable.

For example, let us say your relationship with your family is your number one value. Yet, due to your long work hours, you could barely spend time with them. As a result, your work makes you feel miserable and your mind and body both suffer from the seemingly relentless stress.

The only way to overcome this is to reaffirm your values – or the importance of your family to you and the time to spend with them – so you can make adjustments to your life choices (maybe not taking on so much work or even considering another job?) so that you can live the life you truly want.

As you can see, knowing exactly what your values are will enable you to understand why you make decisions the way you do and live the kind of lifestyle you have. Also, it is important to remember that our values may change over time depending on the experiences we have throughout our lives. Therefore, we should check on our values every so often.

With all these in mind, here are the guidelines that may help you identify the values deep within your inner self. It is best to reflect on them in a peaceful and quiet room, because even background music can affect the way you answer the questions. Also, it is best to have a pen and paper ready so you could jot down the words that you can most identify with in terms of their value to you.

First, think about the happiest moment in your personal life. Visualize the moment in detail in your mind, or you can pick up a photo of that experience to help you remember. Now, answer this question, "What are the factors in this moment in your life that are the reason for making you so happy?"

Now, think about an achievement at school or work you are most proud of. Visualize it in the same way you did with your happiest moment, then when you are ready, answer this second question, "What are the factors in this moment in your career or academic life that contribute to your feelings of success?"

Next, try to recall a moment in your personal life in which

you felt most satisfied, in that you felt at the time that your life is so put together. Now, answer these questions: "What was the thing that you desired then that was fulfilled at the time?" and "why did the satisfaction of that desire give you a sense of fulfillment?" After this, you can do the same for your career or academic life.

After you have answered these questions, take a look at the words you have written as you answered each question.

Then, highlight the words that resonate with values to you (such as ambition, balance, belonging, calm, creativity, compassion, discipline, enjoyment, equality, exploration, faith, family, fun, generosity, happiness, health, independence, intelligence, joy, love, loyalty, order, patriotism, perfection, service, strength, and so on). You can also jot down more words to describe these things you value the most.

Once you have your words, your next step is to rank these values according to their importance to you, starting with the top value. The quickest way to figure that out is by asking yourself, "If I could choose only one value to uphold, which one would it be?" Then, you can take it from there.

Once you have highlighted the values that are closest to your heart, you can then check whether they fit in with the kind of life you have right now as well as your future. Try asking yourself questions such as "Do these values that I currently have made me feel proud of myself?"

"Are these values representative of the things that are important to me, even if they are not so common in this society?" "Can these values contribute to my well-being and those of others?" and so on.

Recognizing and understanding your values is as important as it is challenging because it reveals to you your innermost self. No matter what the results are from this exercise, though, be glad and proud of yourself for taking the steps towards becoming more self-aware.

You can learn so much about yourself, especially your innermost hopes, fears, wishes, and values, by using the power of silence. Hopefully, this will not be the last time that you take a step back and reconnect with your inner self because in the years to come you will continue to transform as a person.

It would be good to know if these changes within you are for the better, not only for yourself but also for the people and things you value in life.

Creating your Quiet Space

Charlotte Eriksson, in a popular quote, said that people need to sit alone in a quiet place sometimes, just "to hear your inner voice", instead of letting it drown in the noise of other people and things.

A quiet space is any place where you can enjoy silence the way you want it, without anyone or anything being able to distract you. It can be somewhere as simple as a corner in your bedroom for short, everyday moments of meditation and peace. Or it can be a special destination that serves as your ultimate getaway for rest and relaxation in times when you really need a high dose of silence.

Whatever the case may be, your quiet space serves as your sanctuary where you can listen to your inner self, contemplate on deep questions, and create freely without the influence of outside criticism and judgment.

Not everyone can afford to regularly buy a ticket to an exotic vacation away from the hustle and bustle, of course, so this chapter is dedicated to helping you to find or create your very own quiet space so that you can afford to enjoy to your heart's desire the power of silence.

Designate a "White Space"

The term "white space" originally refers to a blank section of a document that helps keep the texts, illustrations, and other contents organized and separated. Here, white space is a private and quiet spot where you can find solace in solitude and silence, away from the noise in your life.

It is the quintessential place for catharsis as it allows you to talk to yourself aloud, write in your journal, paint, read, meditate, and so on without anyone disturbing you or making you feel self-conscious.

Designating a white space could be easy if you lived alone; your entire apartment or home can serve as your white space. However, it would be a bit more challenging for those who share a place with other people.

If you happen to be in such a situation and you cannot seem to find any white space elsewhere outside your home, one thing you can do is to determine the time of the day when you do have your home to yourself. It is during these times when your place transforms into your white space.

You can make your white space cozy based on how you define comfort and security. Some people like to visually separate their white space from the other parts of their home by hanging up a curtain.

Others like to evoke a meditative atmosphere by hanging tapestries and keeping candles so they could light them each time they enter their white space. Other people like to keep their white space blank such as by keeping an entire corner bare because they find the simplicity of emptiness soothing to their minds.

You could even create a little ritual for your moments of silence if that brings you happiness and comfort. For example, you can put your phone on silent or airplane mode, or better yet put it away, right before you enter your white space.

You can also ease yourself into a more quiet and peaceful mood by doing 5 to 10 minutes of meditation or write a few pages in your journal once you are within your white space. Silent contemplation can also be had with a hot cup of tea or as you stare at the blank wall. However you wish to keep your white space, what matters is it inspires you to seek silence each time you visit it.

Let Go of Clutter

The thing about noise is it is not limited to sounds alone, for clutter can also have the same effect as noise to your brain. Some people talk about thriving in clutter, but if they know exactly where to find which item regardless of how much stuff they have in a room, then it is not really cluttered, as clutter is defined as a confused jumble of things.

When you look at clutter, your mind is filled with chaos or unwanted thoughts and emotions caused by the sheer disorder.

The idea of having to clean up and organize the clutter seems overwhelming, which is why a lot of people tend to leave the clutter as is, or at least until they "find the time" to deal with them. However, clutter can be dealt with right away, and all the more urgently so if it is starting to cloud your thoughts and affect your mood.

Sorting through the clutter is easy if you approach it in three steps: Round Up, Sort, and Assign a Spot. This simple process is therapeutic in the sense that you will be compelled to let go of unessential items, and so it also causes you to let go of the baggage that comes with them.

Rounding up means gathering all of the items into one spot so the spot that was once filled with clutter now becomes completely bare, a fresh start. With all the things rounded up, you can then move on to sorting through them.

As you go through each item, consider whether you have used it in the last 3 months. Alternatively, think about whether you would consider buying it again if you came across it. If you do, then assign it a spot in the bare space.

For all the items that you no longer use and would not consider buying, you can gather them into one of two boxes: the donate pile, where the items are still perfectly functioning but no longer serve their purpose in your life; and the recycle pile, or the broken items that could no longer serve their purpose at all.

As soon as you have finished decluttering, you should then immediately drop them off to their designated places so they cannot crawl back into your space.

Once all the clutter has been cleared away from your space, you can go ahead and spend more than a few quiet minutes admiring your work. Enjoy the feeling of happiness one can only get from feeling a sense of ownership towards a beautifully clean and organized space. You could even take this moment express gratitude for the things that you currently own.

After all, not everyone can afford to own the things they want to have. You can also express gratitude for the things that you are letting go, because they have indeed served their purpose at some point in your life. Even the ones that you had impulsively bought and never used served the purpose of making you feel happy the moment you picked them up at the shopping center.

Deep Clean your Space

Aside from removing the unessential items, you can also deep clean your space so it will be refreshed. It is important for your quiet space to be neat and clean space as well, because a clean space contributes to good health of both body and mind.

To deep clean your space, all you need to do is to thoroughly clean everything, even the areas you do not usually touch when you quickly clean your home. The best part about this is you can conduct this simultaneously with decluttering, and the perfect time to do it is right after you have rounded up the items and before you assign a spot for each of the ones you will be choosing.

Since deep cleaning consists of routine tasks, you would be able to use this as a moment to enjoy silence as well. This works especially for those who are not particularly comfortable with staying still for long periods of time as they could not help but keep their hands busy.

Decorate with Peace in Mind

If you want a home office that makes you feel more productive, a kitchen that motivates you to prepare healthy meals, and a bedroom that encourages you to enjoy deep sleep, then the look of your quiet space should be one that evokes peace and quiet.

Each person will certainly have a different take on what can be defined as "peaceful" and "quiet." For some, this would be a minimalist approach, with bare walls and a simple but comfortable cushion on the floor. For others, an empty space looks more cold and isolated than warm and relaxing, so they would prefer a cozy couch with shelves full of books to be the things in their quiet space.

That being said, you should also take into consideration the huge impact of lighting. For instance, some people prefer their windows open, but others like their quiet space to be dark.

Probably you can try borrowing a page from the Danes who value their hygge, which roughly refers to the quality of comfort and coziness, by lighting candles and using lamps with warm bulbs instead of an overhead light whenever you want to use your quiet space.

So, now that you know how to create a quiet space, can you immediately think of a special spot in your home that you can "officially" declare as your own version of what it is? Make this project of transforming that space into one that embraces peace and quiet, because the journey towards creating this special sanctuary is just as therapeutic and relaxing as indulging in the end result itself.

Simplifying your Daily Life

Lin Yutang said that the wisdom of light includes getting rid of the non-essentials. When you simplify your daily life, you make everything in it much easier, quieter, and more balanced, and you can do that by reducing whatever keeps it complicated.

It might seem like such as a big task to have to eliminate things from your life, but in reality, you can actually achieve this in little steps. And besides, the process of simplifying your life should also be simple in and of itself, which can be done by taking things day by day, slowly and mindfully.

You can be as creative and resourceful as you can be when you wish to make your daily life simpler and easier. Just keep in mind, though, that this also means making a few sacrifices.

For example, if you are overworking yourself to earn a lot more money, you might want to reconsider by spending less money instead. That way, you would not have to be too exhausted all the time.

Likewise, you might also have to sacrifice some relationships in your life that are doing you more harm than good, such as with a nosy friend who hogs at least an hour of your time on the phone just for the sake of gossip. It could also mean letting go of things that are cluttering up in your home, even if they have some sort of sentimental value to you.

With all these being said, here are some of the steps you can implement right now to help make your daily routines more quiet and relaxed:

Make Mornings and Evenings Relaxing

You simply cannot control every aspect of your day, but you sure can do something about when and how you spend your time after you wake up and before you go to bed. With this in mind, think about how you can make the start and end of each day more relaxing, peaceful, and motivating for you.

This is especially important to those whose daily lives are filled with so much work and interactions with other people as well as those who live in the city and is always surrounded by movement and noise.

Now, if you are looking for ways to make your mornings simpler so you can usher in the day with a bright, fresh, and positive mindset, one tip to try is to drink water as soon as you wake up.

This will instantly awaken your internal system and at the same time refresh your cells after hours of water deprivation during sleep. You can keep a covered glass of cool water on your bedside table the night before so it will be an effortless habit to keep.

When it comes to rejuvenating your body, you could do yourself a big favor by doing a few simple stretches in bed or right after you get out of it. Stretching wakes up your muscles and boosts your blood flow. Moreover, by doing stretches every morning, you can condition your muscles and joints to be more limber.

Another thing to incorporate into a simple morning routine is to have essentially the same healthy breakfast every day.

For instance, you can have oatmeal every morning for breakfast, and then just add variety on the add-ons, such as pairing it with the fruits of the season and different savory sides such as hard-boiled egg on Mondays, tofu bacon on Tuesdays, and so on. This might sound a bit extreme, but it will really help you out as it eliminates the trouble of having to decide on what to have for breakfast.

As for your night routine, some great habits to incorporate are to detach yourself from your digital devices at least an hour or two before you go to bed, write out your thoughts in a journal, and practice deep relaxation meditation (entire chapters are dedicated to these tips, so let us not get into detail).

You can also do the things that make you feel more comfortable and relaxed so as to set the mood for sleep. For some, it could be journaling, while for others, it could be writing down a to-do list for the following day. It also helps to take a multivitamin before bed, especially if you are certain that your diet does not really allow you to get your complete required set of vitamins and minerals.

A warm shower or bath one hour before bedtime can also soothe your tired muscles and be quite therapeutic to a stressed out mind. Right after doing so, it would also be ideal to step into a cool, dark, and silent bedroom for it will surely encourage sleep.

However you want to spend your mornings and evenings, the bottom-line is to keep your plan simple enough for you to follow through with it consistently. If there is any aspect of your routine that you feel is cluttering things up, then consider eliminating it or reducing it to a level that is much more comfortable for you.

Streamline your Schedule

Most, if not all, of us, want to do more in less time, but if you want to be efficient and effective without sacrificing your sanity, then what you can do is to take better control over your time each day. This is made easy when you streamline your schedule or, in other words, organize your tasks for the day based on when and for how long you plan to do each.

It is so important to simplify and streamline your schedule because – let's face it – we all have a limited amount of time on our hands. That being said, the first thing to take into consideration before you start mapping out your schedule is the number of hours you have for the day.

For instance, if you need to be in bed by 10 p.m. and awake by 6 a.m. on most days, then that means out of the 24 hours you have, you should deduct 8 hours of sleep. Thus, you are left with 16 hours of waking time which you should then carefully allocate to the right activities.

You can streamline your schedule using a pen and paper or an app on a digital device, but regardless of the medium you choose to use, it is best to do it in a quiet room where not even music can affect your stream of thoughts.

If you are new to this idea, here are some tips on how you can streamline your schedule each day:

Choose a Time of the Day for Scheduling

This might sound overboard, but you really should make an appointment with yourself for scheduling, because by doing so you are making it an unavoidable part of your day. Your schedule will minimize your chances of procrastinating as well as biting off more than you can chew, so scheduling should definitely become a habit.

Some people prefer to plan their day early in the morning, shortly before or after breakfast, because it helps set the right mood for the rest of the day. Others like it better before they go to bed so that when they wake up in the morning they would know exactly what needs to be done.

Once you have decided on the time when you can schedule, you should then determine how long it would take you to plan. Most of the time, it takes 15 to 30 minutes, but you can go with what works for you. You can even use an alarm to remind you to start scheduling, and a timer to prevent you from over-planning.

Recognize your Top Priorities

Before you stuff your day with tasks, think first about the most important task you need to accomplish. Reflect briefly on it is your priority above all the others, and how you would be able to dedicate most of your energy on it for that day. Only after you have set your schedule for that task should you then focus on the remaining ones.

If you have too many tasks in mind, you can write them all down and then make quick adjustments based on your personal needs and preferences. One simple way to do this is to highlight the top three tasks and cross off the unimportant ones. If a task is important but is something you can reschedule to another day or delegate to someone else, then make a note of them.

With this in mind, you would be able to realize the importance of saying "no" to tasks that only add burden to you. Of course, if it is a task that you have agreed upon as a favor to someone and if it is worth the sacrifice of your personal time and energy because this person is important to you, then it should not be considered an irrelevant task.

Focus on One Task at a Time

Multitasking is a fallacy because we are certainly incapable of focusing on more than one task at the same time. Rather, what we do is to switch rapidly from one task to another, and while this might seem efficient at first, it will certainly make you feel more exhausted and it could cause your output to be a lot more "quantity" than "quality."

You can definitely do yourself a big favor by focusing on only one task at a time, and to not stop until you have reached your desired level of progress on the task before you switch to another one.

Time blocking is a great scheduling strategy to apply if your goal is to ensure that you will practice the habit of single-tasking. To do this, all you need to do is to assign a specific period of time for a specific task, or a specific day for a particular project.

For example, if your goal is to have a fixed morning routine, then you can time block 6 to 7 a.m. for your early morning exercise and a quick shower.

Then, you can time block 7:30 a.m. to 9 a.m. for breakfast, getting ready for work, and commuting to the office. After that, you can time block your 9 to 5 specifically for appointments at work, before you time block 5 to 6 p.m. for the commute back to your home, and so on.

The great thing about streamlining your schedule is it will simplify your day. At the same time, it will enable you to see an overview of exactly when you have free time and for how long. Moreover, it will sharpen your focus on the task that has been time blocked because that particular time-frame is the only period you have for it.

All in all, the quickest way to simplify your day is to identify and get rid of anything that does not serve a meaningful purpose to your life. That way, you can eliminate bad habits such as spending too much time on social media, idle chatter and overworking on projects where you are underpaid.

At the same time, you can dedicate more of your time and energy of the day on exercise, cooking healthy meals at home, and enjoying quality periods of quiet and rest.

4 - Unplugging from the Digital Noise

"We get sucked into the Internet and streaming information, and it's time to just unplug and look within."

Jonathan Cain

Nowadays, much of the noise most of us experience actually comes from our digital devices. More specifically, they come from all of the input we could get from whatever it is we had downloaded into our phones or computers – games, e-books, and so on – or the internet. Take a look at your social media feed, for instance, because you can clearly see how bombarded it is with information.

Yet, most of what you see is not actually relevant to you or is something you care for.

Be that as it may, because we so yearn to find something – anything – that we might just find to be interesting or useful to us, we continue to scroll down and down until we perhaps encounter something that is someone funny or thought-provoking or concerning, that we would feel a sense of accomplishment for having come across it.

Little do most of us know, all of these texts, pictures, videos, sounds, and other sensory input contribute to information overload or overexposure to data or information.

Information overload has a lot of negative effects, and according to sociologist Georg Simmel, it could cause people to become exhausted too easily, to the point where they could no longer respond effectively to new situations. Moreover, being overexposed to data leads to poor decision-making because, let's face it, most of us can only process a limited amount of information at a time.

On the other hand, writer, teacher, and consultant Clay Shirky states that we do not suffer from information overload; rather, he calls it "filter failure."

In other words, we cannot really blame the fact that all the information is within reach now, thanks to our digital devices, but what we can do to solve the problem of information overload is to control what kind of information we allow ourselves to access when we should access them, and how.

That said, we should designate a certain time of the day to remove ourselves from the vortex of information overload via a digital detox.

A "digital detox" is a specific time-frame in which you do not make use of any electronic devices – be it your phone, your computer, the television, and so on – for the primary purpose of reducing stress, lowering anxiety, and enhancing your appreciation of the physical world. A digital detox is a perfect time to enjoy the power of silence as well.

Multiple studies can support the notion that doing this regularly can increase your mental health, boost your emotional intelligence, enhance your relationships with the people around you, increase your productivity, and even improve your body posture.

Of course, it is up to you on when and for how long you should do it, but if you are looking for some guidelines and tips, here are some great ways on how to make the most out of your digital detox:

Highlight the Why

Do you think going on a digital detox is important to you? If you do, then ask yourself what your reasons behind it are.

Some people do it because they want to enhance their creativity and productivity, and mindless noise on the television or the internet is keeping them from hearing themselves think.

Others want to go on a digital detox because seeing all the updates from their friends on social media is causing them to become more and more envious, and this sense of self-awareness is telling them to take charge before it gets any worse.

There are also those who wish to enjoy the time they could spend with the people who are actually right next beside them, but their digital devices are keeping them from being in the present moment.

Find out what your motivations are for wanting to go on a digital detox because these will help you stick to your schedule no matter how tempting it is to stay hooked.

Identify your Digital Detox Time

Some people can afford to just spontaneously decide to go on a digital detox for 24 to 48 hours, but for others, this can be unrealistic, especially if their work requires them to go online every now and then. Whatever your case may be, it would be best to choose a specific time-frame for you to go on a digital detox.

For instance, if you know for a fact that you do not really need to go online and check your work email after 5 pm, then your digital detox can start there. You can also treat your days off as digital detox times.

The first hour of your day, or right from the moment you wake up, is a good time to go on a digital detox. Let this be a quiet moment with nothing but you and your thoughts as you prepare your breakfast, shower, and do all of the other things that need to be done to start your day right.

At least an hour before your bedtime is also a good time to start a digital detox because this will not only give you the peace and quiet you so need to be in the mood for sleep but also prevent you from developing insomnia. This is because the blue light emitted from a digital screen tricks the brain into thinking it is still daytime, thus preventing you from transitioning to sleep mode.

An alternative way to do a digital detox is to set a daily limit for the time you spend on your devices, instead of scheduling a period for your detox. This strategy is especially helpful to some people because it makes them become more selective of the kind of information they choose online as well as how they interact with their devices.

This is also effective for those whose work actually requires them to use digital devices, such as online writers and computer programmers because their limit will cause them to focus much of their "plugged in" time on work.

Keep in mind that you can always reschedule your digital detox depending on your needs and preferences. What matters is you stick to it regularly.

Develop Digital Detox Habits

Aside from setting a schedule, another way to reduce the amount of time you spend on your digital devices is to develop specific habits that will eventually make it effortless for you to do so. To help you get started, here are some common digital detox habits that you can apply to your life right now:

No Phones during Mealtimes

Put away your smartphone during mealtimes, regardless of whether you are eating alone or with family. You can even talk to your family and friends about this and practice "phone stacking," or putting all of your devices in a box or in the middle of the table before the meal.

You can even come up with rules to help impose this habit, such as by footing the bill or buying desserts for everyone if you are the first person to pick your phone up before meal-time is over.

No Text, No Call while Driving

Keep is to put your phone on silent mode and store it away while you are driving. This will save not just your life one day, but others on the road, too. Understand that no phone call could be so important that you would risk it all just to answer it.

"Screen Free" Bed

A really good habit to keep is to make your bed a "screen free" zone, in that you will not ever bring your phone or your laptop, or any other digital device to it. Give it a try and you will notice that you will sleep much better later on. Besides, if you are using your phone as an alarm clock you will be more likely to get out of bed if it is not within reach as soon as it wakes you up.

From these habits, you can also start coming up with your own to reduce the amount of time you spend each day in front of a screen.

Make your Digital Detox Enjoyable

There are so many great activities you could engage in while on a digital detox, the most invigorating of which is to commune with nature. Since an entire chapter in this book is dedicated to that, it will not be discussed in detail here. Aside from it, here are some of the ways in which you can enjoy your digital detox:

Enjoy an "at home" spa

Indulging in some "me" time during a digital detox does not have to cost a lot of money. In fact, more people have been recreating the spa-like treatment within the comforts of their own home.

One way you can do that is to dim the lights, light some scented candles, run a warm bath, pop into it a bath bomb, and then soak yourself for a few minutes in its rejuvenating waters. As you do, you can take your time exfoliating your skin, deep conditioning your hair, and all of the other "spa" things people do. You can also pour yourself a glass of wine and just enjoy this still and quiet moment.

Re-visit your favorite books

Sometimes, we get so caught up with the happenings in the digital arena that we forget the nostalgic charm we used to enjoy when we read paperbacks. But if we take the time to put down our phones and open those old books again, we could transport ourselves back to the old, familiar world that once enraptured us.

The beautiful thing about re-reading your old favorites from so many years ago is that you would be able to interpret the messages and stories in them now that your mindset and perspectives in life have changed. So, go ahead and cuddle up with your favorite book and the drink you used to enjoy while reading it in a quiet and cool corner, even just for an hour or two.

Try doodling or sketching

Making art is a cheap and easy way to relax, let your creative juices flow, and enjoy peace and quiet. You can express yourself in any way you wish through your sketches, paintings, colors, pencils, and all your other art media in a quiet library or peaceful park.

One benefit to putting away your digital devices and turning to more traditional forms of art is it helps enhance your focus and reduce your stress levels at the same time. Your work can also represent the thoughts and feelings coming from deep within your inner self.

Some would even scribble for a few minutes with their eyes closed because this helps them loosen up as well as get to know another side of themselves. If you want to give this a try, here is how you can do it:

Get a piece of paper and tape its edges against a table. Grab a box of crayons and place it somewhere that makes it easy for you to reach them. When you are ready, take a few deep breaths to relax before you grab a crayon. Then, close your eyes and allow your hands to just scribble to your heart's desire. After you are done with your "eyes closed" scribble, you can go ahead and examine your output.

Aside from these simple but relaxing activities that you can do without a digital device, there are plenty of other suggestions to explore throughout this book. But as you can see, going on a digital detox is something everyone can look forward to each day. Enjoy silence just as much as you enjoy your digital detox, and your mind and heart will be truly filled.

5 - Introspecting through Journaling

"In the journal, I do not just express myself more openly than I could to any person; I create myself."

Susan Sontag

Everyone experiences ups and downs in life, regardless of whether they would define theirs as simple or complex. There are happy times just as there are sad, moments of anger just as there are of love and plenty of other emotions and experiences in between.

All these cannot be avoided, but sometimes it is important to take a step back from these so as to not feel overwhelmed. It is during these moments of "stepping back" that we are able to keep ourselves from being consumed by the noise of life.

It is a quiet time when we can reconnect with our true passions and goals and truly get to know our inner selves. And in these moments, we can appreciate the power of silence.

One of the most effective ways to release all of your emotions and clarify most if not all of your thoughts, in true silence that is free from distraction, is through journaling. To keep a journal means to write regularly in a notebook everything that crosses your mind. Susan Sontag said that you are creating your own self when you write a journal, more than expressing yourself.

Most of the time, people record their daily experiences in a journal, while others stick to a certain "theme" by writing only poems or songs, or doodling, or retelling only the highlights of their life in their journal.

If you have not started journaling yet, or if you used to and had forgotten how good it was for you, then it helps to know that it is really good for your mental and emotional well-being.

For instance, regular writing helps spark creativity as well as enhances your concentration. Writing out your thoughts and emotions is therapeutic as well, in the sense that it enables you to "transfer" them from your mind to paper.

The best part about journaling is there are no judgments. You are free to write whatever is on your mind. There is no standard set of criteria to determine whether you are doing a good job of journaling or not. In a way, it is a lot like meditation, because what matters is you are doing it.

Of course, you are more likely to write your thoughts smoothly the more frequently you write, but it is okay if you still struggle to put into words how you feel no matter how many entries you have made.

That being said, you might still be looking for ideas on how you can start keeping a journal. Here are some guidelines that you can turn to, but again, you are free to approach your experience in journaling in any way you prefer.

Paper, Digital, or Online

Back then, people were only able to journal on paper, but now you can choose whether to write in a paper notebook, in a device, or via a blog.

When it comes to journaling on paper, there is something romantic about writing in a secret notebook that you can hide away in your sock drawer, and there is something comforting about seeing your thoughts being translated into written words in your own handwriting.

Using the digital medium for journaling can also have its benefits. For one, you can keep thousands of entries in a single device instead of having to buy paper notebooks each time.

You can also easily search for a previous entry just by typing in some keywords and then letting the device pull them up for you, in case you want to go back on a quote you wrote or a memory you had recorded from long ago. The biggest setback with a digital diary, though, is if something happens to your device. In such cases, all your entries would get wiped out.

If you are not fond of writing on paper and you are worried about losing your device, then what you can do is journal online. Some people like to keep a secret blog in which they remain anonymous as they post all of their thoughts and emotions online.

Others like to keep their entries in a password encrypted drive, which means they can access their journal anywhere and would not have to worry about losing their entries in case their device crashes. The only thing they could worry about is if they get hacked.

No matter what type of medium you choose for journaling, the bottom-line is it can help you to enjoy being in the midst of silence as you release your thoughts and emotions from your mind to it. Journaling should always be a source of comfort and joy for anyone, after all.

Try Journaling Prompts

Currently, there are plenty of special journaling products that contain "prompts" – questions or quotes that inspire you to start writing. You can start with those if you always find yourself at a loss for words whenever you try to start an entry. You can also try answering any one of the following journaling prompts below each time you wish to write something:

Prompts for Discovering your Inner Self

What is the one memory in your mind that brings so much nostalgia to your heart? Describe the memory by engaging all your senses: what you see, hear, smell, feel, and even taste.

- Write a letter to your future self (your 20 years older self, perhaps?). Describe what life is like right now, especially what you are currently into, who are the people you spend most of your time with, and so on.

- Write a letter to your past self (yourself 10 years ago, maybe?). Talk about how far you have gone now and how much you have accomplished so far your passions, and the important people in your life.

- Confess the worst thing you have ever done, and how you feel about it. Write about what you can do to forgive yourself for this transgression.

- Write about your biggest but most secret desire. Why do you want it so much and is it possible for you to acquire it?

- Write about the craziest thing you have ever done in your whole life. Describe it in detail and explain why you think it is crazy.

- What is on your mind right now? Write down what you think of it, how you feel about it, and what you can do about it.

Prompts to Boost Productivity

- What is your biggest achievement in life and how were you able to do it? Why do you think this moment in your life made you feel successful?

- Describe your biggest life goal in vivid detail. Explain your reason for having this goal, then write down what you need to achieve first before you can acquire it, how much time you think it will take you to achieve it, and so on.

- When do you feel most productive? Why do you think it is that particular time? What have you been able to achieve during those times?

- What do you think you need to do in order to move closer towards achieving your goal?

- What are your top five biggest strengths that can help you achieve your goal? How would you be able to wield each of them to do this?

- Think of someone successful that you have always looked up to. What qualities do they have that make them so admirable? What were the struggles they had to go through before they achieved success in life?

- When was the last time you got distracted? What could be the reason behind it? What can you do to avoid this distraction in the future?

Prompts for Relaxation and Peace of Mind

- What has been causing you an unusual level of stress

lately? Write each of them down, and then explain why they are your source of stress and what you can do reduce them in your life.

- Make a list of all the people and things that make you feel happy. Express gratitude for each of these. Choose from the list the ones that are closest to your heart and describe in detail your fondest memory of them.

- "If you want to forget something or someone, never hate it, or never hate him/her. Everything and everyone that you hate is engraved upon your heart; if you want to let go of something, if you want to forget, you cannot hate." What do you make of this quote by C. Joybell C.?

- When was the last time you truly felt rested and relaxed? Do you think you need more of these? How would you be able to get enough of it?

- Think about a specific area near you that immediately evokes peace and relaxation the moment you think of it (you could even print out a picture of it and paste it in your journal). Why qualities of this place make it so? When would you be able to visit this place?

- Write about how you would like to spend a day free from responsibilities. Where would you like to go? Who will you spend time with? What will you do? How will you feel by the end of that day?

Prompts for Enhancing your Relationships with Others

- Create a list of all the people in your life who love, support, and accept you wholeheartedly. You could even draw their faces or post a picture of them next to their names. Then, write down your most fond memory with them. If that person is still around think about how you could spend more time with them.

- Write a letter to each of the most important people in your life. If you want to forgive or if you want to be forgiven by that person, how much you appreciate them, miss them, love them, or simply enjoy their everyday company. Let it be as heartfelt as you wish. Sending those letters out is optional, but if you feel that they could enhance your relationship with these people, then, by all means, do so.

- Challenge yourself to come up with a list of 50 ways you could express love and kindness to others, whether they are humans or animals. Then, challenge yourself to try to do one thing on the list every day.

- If you could do one thing for someone else, throw them a surprise party, take them to a nice vacation spot, buy them something they have always wanted, or whatever you think is best for that person, who would it be and what would you do? Plan it in detail. Then, if you wish, you could go ahead and do just that.

- Hopefully, this chapter has inspired you to get into the habit of journaling, even for just 5 minutes per day. The early morning would be a great time to do so because your surroundings would still be peacefully cool and quiet. Writing things down before turning in for the night can also increases your chances of a good night's sleep. Come to think of it, you can journal anytime you wish, for in silence you would not only be able to hear yourself think but write about it, too.

Meditating in Silence

Meditation, in general, is defined as the practice of contemplating deeply and continuously on a particular subject. A growing number of people are practicing meditation, mostly because of the praise it got from famous and successful people, including Steve Jobs, Oprah Winfrey, Richard Gere, and Hugh Jackman, to name a few. Even the big companies have started encouraging their employees to meditate.

Jobs, for instance, allowed his employees at Apple to practice half an hour of meditation during working hours every day and would even sponsor meditation sessions at the office.

One of Google's perks is offering their employees meditation courses because they believe it will improve their mental health as well as their performance at work. Nike also encourages meditation in the workplace and even has relaxation rooms where their employees can practice meditation.

As for the different ways to meditate, there certainly are plenty. However, in this particular case, we will be putting much emphasis on a simple yet highly beneficial and relevant type of meditation, which is to meditate in silence.

The paradox of silent meditation is that the longer you practice it, the more it uncovers a different kind of noise – your innermost thoughts. As a result, you will find that the noise surrounding you each day does not compare to the noise that could be buried deep inside your mind. Be that as it may, it is good to be fully aware of these thoughts and to accept them, for only then would you be able to let them go.

Another paradox of silent meditation is it is not meant to silence the mind. Rather, you are to listen to your mind as it brings to the surface more deep-seated thoughts, feelings, memories, and expectations. By allowing yourself only silence in the outside world, your mind will finally be able to feel honest towards itself.

If you want to give silent meditation a try, here are some great techniques to start with.

6 - Deep Breathing Meditation

Have you ever stopped to appreciate how your body continues to keep you alive by breathing?

This is but one of the questions that arise to mind in most of those who have developed an appreciation for breathing meditation. More importantly, this technique has helped many people lower their anxiety, improve focus, and encourage deep thought.

Breathing meditation can be practiced anywhere, but you will find that it is most effective when done in a quiet and peaceful room. So, give it a try right now by keeping in mind the following steps:

Step 1: Find a quiet space, preferably with fresh air, where no one will disturb you.

A shady area at the park is a great place to do deep breathing meditation, but essentially you can do it anywhere as long as the air is clean and fresh. Once you are in that place, you can sit or lie down comfortably, but make sure to keep your back straight and your shoulders relaxed.

Step 2: Place one hand on your abdomen and the other on your chest.

Doing this will enhance your deep breathing technique because the key is that your abdomen – not your chest – should be the one rising and falling as you take in your deep breaths. By putting one hand on each spot, you can easily determine that.

Step 3: Take a few deep breaths before starting.

While there are no techniques set in stone when it comes to deep breathing, most people still want to have some sort of guideline on how long they should inhale, hold their breath, and exhale.

If you happen to be one of them, then you can try inhaling slowly through your nostrils for 4 seconds until your lungs are completely filled. Then, hold it in for 2 seconds before you slowly exhale through your mouth for a slow 8 seconds.

Practice this technique a few times, and when you are ready, you can proceed to enter the meditative state.

Step 4: Relax your eyelids and concentrate on your breath.

It helps to gently think, I am about to do deep breathing meditation so that you can set the right mood for the session. Begin with your natural breath, then slowly inhale, allowing your mind to focus on the movement of the air as it fills your lungs.

As you hold your breath, concentrate on how your muscles respond to the expansion of your lungs. Notice, in particular, the area around your throat, shoulders, upper back, and chest. It should not be painful.

As you exhale, trace the breath as it leaves your body and dissipates into the air. Give yourself a second or two to relax before you move on to the next inhale.

Step 5: Relax your body with each deep breath.

As you continue to breathe deeply, notice if there is any tension in any part of your body. Once you spot one, imagine each breath being concentrated in that area. Continue to "breathe into" that spot until it starts to relax. You can also visualize the tension leaving your body as you exhale.

Step 6: Relax your mind with each deep breath.

After your body is completely relaxed, gently shift your focus towards your mind. Observe your mind as if you are a person looking in, and notice if there is any tension or disturbance in it.

If you do notice a disturbing thought, a painful feeling, or anything that strains your mind, breathe deeply and visualize these thoughts exiting your body with each exhale. Continue to do so until your mind feels completely light and at peace.

When you are ready to come out of deep breathing meditation, do not make the end abrupt. Instead, draw yourself out of it by gently reverting back to your natural breath. Give yourself a few minutes to relax in natural breathing as well before you stand up and go about your day.

7 - Five Minutes of Silent Meditation

This simple technique can be practiced by any beginner to meditation, but what makes it so thought-provoking is how it can actually give you a fresh perspective on time. The only way to understand it is to practice it yourself, but before you begin make sure to have a clock or your watch close by. Now, here are the steps:

Step 1: Settle in your quiet space.

You may sit down on a chair or on a cushion on the floor. Keep a straight back but maintain relaxed shoulders. You can shift around until you find a position that is comfortable for you.

Step 2: Ease yourself into the meditative state.

Before the start of the meditation, check the time. As soon as a new minute starts, close your eyes and quietly think, "I am about to meditate for five minutes." Then, focus on your natural breath.

Step 3: Allow yourself to be open and curious.

As you continue to focus on your breath, notice how your mind reacts. It might start to think about how long it has been since you started, when the three minutes is up, and so on. Whatever thoughts cross your mind, let them fade away until you can draw yourself back to the sensation of your natural breath.

Step 4: Gently ease yourself out of the meditative state once you think the five minutes are up.

Continue to focus on your breath until you cannot help but think that it has indeed been five minutes. Once you feel that the time is up, you can gently open your eyes and check the clock or watch.

Step 5: Determine whether you were able to end the meditation at the right time.

As soon as you have opened your eyes, check to see if you really were able to meditate for exactly five minutes based solely on your intuition.

However, it does not really matter whether you stopped at exactly minutes or not because what really matters is how it allows you to really stop and reflect on your perspective of time. With more practice, you will be able to sharpen your intuition on time as well as develop an appreciation of the present moment and the fleeting of time itself.

You can start practicing silent meditation during your quiet time and in your quiet space, but eventually, you will learn to practice it anywhere and at any time of the day. For instance, you can spend even just 5 minutes of your 15-minute break at work on it, or you can practice it before you go to bed at night.

Regardless of the length of your meditation, though, what matters is you do it regularly. That way, your mind will always have its moment of clarity no matter how noisy or busy your life can get.

8 - Connecting with Nature

Silence in the midst of nature has got to be the most beautiful way to relax and get away from the noise of life, even for just a little while. In fact, it has been scientifically proven that nature can heal the mind and body in many ways. Rachel Carson couldn't have said it any better than those who stop to appreciate the beauty of the earth, become more energized and they find the strength that lasts a lifetime.

For instance, getting a healthy dose of sunlight outdoors will grant you your much-needed vitamin D, which helps strengthen your bones and teeth by improving your body's ability to absorb calcium. Moreover, vitamin D is a natural mood booster as it reduces blood pressure and enhances blood flow.

Aside from the sunshine, you can also inhale as much fresh air as you want in nature. This is in stark contrast to the polluted and stuffy air you would usually get in the city, which causes the lungs to work twice as hard just to get the oxygen from it.

It is also good to know that serotonin or the neurotransmitter that is responsible for your memory, mood, and social behavior is directly linked to the amount of oxygen in your body. If your serotonin levels are low, you will feel sluggish and even depressed.

But since nature's fresh air makes it almost effortless for your lungs to get the oxygen it needs, your serotonin levels will become regulated and you will feel much more relaxed and happy. With this in mind, it would be a good idea for you to practice deep breathing while you are in nature so you can make the most of the clean air.

Being in nature also helps reduce the stress you would naturally get from the demands of your daily routine. You can maximize this by engaging in some fun activities while in nature to also increase the level of endorphins in your system. Endorphin is another neurochemical that can boost your mood when the brain is triggered to produce it.

Now, some may already agree with all of these, but if you are the type of person who is so used to the urban landscape, then now is the time to give the great outdoors a try. To give you some ideas, here are some ways on how you can immerse in the power of silence by connecting with nature:

Go trail running or riding

Trail running, also called fell or mountain running is the name of a sport wherein you would run and hike over trails. Trail riding is also done in the same terrain, except you are crossing the trail on a mountain bike instead of on foot. Most places have a safe and controlled nature park where people can follow a trail for the purpose of exercise.

If you want to know the trails in your area, you can ask your local running or biking clubs and stores as well as national park offices. You can also ask your friends on social media because at least one of them might just be a running enthusiast.

Trail running and riding are great ways to get a lot of oxygen into your system while enjoying the natural scenery. Just make sure that the trail you have chosen for this activity is secure before you start. Also, if you are new to the area it would be advisable for you to invite some friends to come with you or to bring your dog and for you to go there in the early morning rather than the evening.

To make your trail running experience truly enjoyable, wear shoes that are built for the trail, because you will be encountering some mud, puddles, roots, rocks, and other such materials across the terrain and regular running shoes might not be able to handle them. Always bring some water with you and put on sunscreen before you go out as well as some bug repellant.

Swim in the lake or at the beach

If you are fortunate enough to be living close to a beach or lake, then you should certainly make the most of it. Swimming leisurely in a natural pool of water, that is guaranteed safe, of course, is another great way to enjoy peace and quiet in the midst of nature.

The beach, for instance, is the quintessential picture of relaxation. Enjoy the natural sound of the waves crashing against the shore or, better yet, swim in deep if you know how and enjoy the peaceful stillness below.

You could even wear a pair of goggles so you can enjoy watching the world of corals, fishes, and sea plants underneath. Just take care not to go swimming without a life guard unless you are a certified professional.

Try Cloud Gazing or Bird Watching

Wherever you may be, you can certainly enjoy such simple

outdoor activities as cloud gazing and bird watching. All you ever really need is a nearby plain where you can spread out a nice blanket, lie down, and look up at the skies.

You could even bring a little picnic basket of goodies with you to make the experience more fun. This might sound a bit cheesy, but the opportunity to take pleasure in such activities is being taken for granted by most of us who are so hooked to our computers.

If you want to give cloud gazing a try, you would be glad to know that there is actually a meditation practice called Sky Gazing, because it uses the sky as a metaphor of one's state of mind while practicing it.

You can even liken the noise in your life – your worries, anxieties, and bad memories – to clouds and your mind as the sky, in that they do cross the sky but they never really stay there. Be on the lookout for clouds that embody certain thoughts that cross your mind, and then watch them float away and take those troublesome thoughts along with them.

As for bird-watching, all you really need is a good pair of binoculars, some quality time for solitude, and a regional field guide to help you identify the local birds. The wonderful thing about this activity is you will learn to appreciate different species of birds and really become more in tune with life in nature.

Give it a try once or twice, with a borrowed pair of binoculars, at the park or in any nature spot where you are likely to find different kinds of birds. For starters, you will be able to find songbirds within the first two hours after the sun rises and before the sun sets. If you are a big fan of eagles and hawks, in particular, then you should be on the lookout for them before the crack of dawn.

Remember to be very quiet because you might scare them away. If you find yourself being more drawn to this activity, you could even join a birding group so you can all silently enjoy the experience of bird watching together.

You do not have to spend a lot of money to enjoy nature of course, although there is definitely nothing wrong with going on a great nature getaway. It is just as pleasurable to enjoy a sunny picnic, meditate, or read a good book underneath a shady tree at the park, or hop on a bus to a nearby beach.

Find the time to connect with nature and enjoy the silence there, for only then would you be able to appreciate that the world – and all its wonder – is much bigger than all of your problems combined.

9 - Rekindling the Joy of Reading

"To acquire the habit of reading is to construct for yourself a refuge from almost all the miseries of life."

W. Somerset Maugham

Most adults, even those who would describe themselves to be readers when they were younger, now struggle to find the time to fully immerse themselves in a good book. Sometimes, they would buy a book and "read" it because they feel that they should, or because it is a popular piece with an upcoming movie adaptation.

However, all too often people end up not finishing the books they have started to read or, worse, only skim through the book instead of allowing it to transport them to the universe contained within its pages as it should.

If you have lost your genuine love for reading or if you have never been a reader, then it is time to use the power of silence to rekindle your joy of it. Here are the best strategies you can apply right now to find true pleasure in reading without getting distracted by the noise of the outside world:

Dedicate a Special Quiet Place and Time for Reading

If you think you do not have enough time for pleasurable reading, then the solution is to make time for it. Set an appointment with yourself just to enjoy a good story, whether it is on the weekend or an hour before bedtime, and then stick to it.

Let your quiet space be your little reading nook as well so that each time you enter it you would be motivated to pick up where you left off in the story. Former bookworms also find that they are more drawn back to the world of books each time they enter an old library, so if you want you can also become a member of one and then spend your quiet time there, just for reading.

Start with Short Fiction

Truth be told, not everyone has the luxury of time to read an entire novel, for all avid readers, know that the best way to read a good novel is to not stop until it is finished. If you happen to be someone who could spare only a short amount of time and energy on reading, then your next best adventure to take aside from a novel would be in the form of short stories.

Short stories typically have less than 8,000 words, which means that an average person can finish reading it within 45 minutes. The best part is that there are thousands of free short stories online, and all you have to do is browse through the list of titles based on your favorite genre.

If you are looking for some ideas, here is a list of some of the most profound classic and modern short fiction stories and books to try:

- The Most Dangerous Game by Richard Connell (1924)

- The Lottery by Shirley Jackson (1948)

- A Good Man is Hard to Find by Flannery O'Connor (1953)

- A Sound of Thunder by Ray Bradbury (1952)

- The Tell-Tale Heart by Edgar Allan Poe (1843)

- A Very Short Story by Ernest Hemingway (1924)

- The Celebrated Jumping Frog of Calaveras County by Mark Twain (1865)

- Interpreter of Maladies by Jhumpa Lahiri (1999)

- Seven Lives to Repay Our Country by Edward H. Carpenter (2011)

- Home by Alice Munro (2006)

- In Hindsight by Callan Wink (2015)

- What Happened to the Baby? By Cynthia Ozick (2006)

Stop and Move On

This might sound sacrilegious to hardcore readers out there, but if you are reading a story, book, or article that you simply do not find interesting, then, by all means, stop reading it and move on to another one. Even the best authors cannot please everyone, so no matter how much others have been raving about a particular book. Drop it if you yourself cannot find pleasure in its characters, theme, and plot.

That being said, it is also a good idea to try to explore beyond your comfort zone of genres every now and then. For instance, if all you have been reading since childhood is sci-fi, then maybe you could also try historical fiction.

If you are fond of adventure, you might also discover that you actually find satire enjoyable. Just continue to explore more pieces until you find ones that really make you want to read more deeply each day.

Go Back to Paper Books

While digital books can save you storage space and money, it simply cannot beat the old world charm of reading paper books. Of course, this does not mean you should cut out e-books entirely. Rather, it would help your mind and eyes to read paper books every now and then.

One idea to help you find joy in reading again is to buy the latest novel or novella of your favorite author. That way, you know for a fact that you enjoy that author's writing style and the time and money you spend on the paper book is worth the investment.

If you have read all of your favorite author's books and he or she has not published anything lately, or if you have never been fond of reading but would like to start, then you can try the "tested and proven" ones.

In other words, pick up the popular books that are always on the New York Times bestseller list based on the genre that you prefer the most. The good thing about doing this is you will not have to worry about not finding a copy at your local bookstore. In fact, they would most likely be on display themselves.

Reach for Graphic Novels

One "hack" to help you start reading again is to find and enjoy a really well-done graphic novel. Graphic novels are basically books consisting of long fictional work, but instead of the story being told in written form, it is mostly in drawn or comic-strip form, with only the dialogue and bits of narrative in the text.

Graphic novels are great for those who are still easing themselves into the world of reading but are still a bit intimidated by the long sentences and complexity of written stories.

If you are looking for some suggestions, here are some of the best graphic novels to date:

- Batman: The Dark Knight Returns by Frank Miller (1986)

- Watchmen (Titan Edition) (1986)

- The Sandman: Dream country by Neil Gaiman (1991)

- Ant Colony by Michael DeForge (2014)

- Teratoid Heights by Mat Brinkman (2000)

- A Drunken Dream and Other Stories by Moto Hagio (2010)

- Baby Bjornstrand by Renée French (2014)

- The Furry Trap by Josh Simmons (2012)

- Meat Cake Bible by Dame Darcy (2016)

Clearly, there are plenty of paths to take if you want to build the habit of reading for pleasure. And this becomes so much easier the moment you find peace in solitude and silence.

10 - Conclusion

Now that you have reached the end of this book, it is safe to assume that you have developed a deep appreciation for silence and solitude and that you are about to apply some of the things you have just learned into your life if you have not already.

Each time you start to feel overwhelmed by the noise of life, always remember to go back to the pages of this book to remind yourself that you can step away from it all, even just for a bit, through the power of silence.

Try not to be too hard on yourself by spending some quiet time to think and breathe deeply in your quiet space, let out your hopes and fears on paper, enjoy the scent of fresh air and the beauty of nature, and introspect so you can reconnect with your inner self. By spending even just a few minutes in peaceful silence, you can positively impact the rest of your day.

Thank You

As we reach the end of this book, I want to say thanks for reading this book.

I want to get this information out to as many people as possible. If you found this book helpful, I would greatly appreciate you leaving me a review. This helps others find the book as well.

This book was self-published with the amazing help of Self-Publishing Made Easy Now! [3] . You can grab a free copy of the checklist that started my journey here: FREE Self-Publishing Checklist [4] .

[3] https://selfpublishingmadeeasynow.com/xpjv

[4] https://selfpublishingmadeeasynow.com/free_checklist

Disclaimer

This document is geared towards providing exact and reliable information in regards to the topic and issue covered. The publication is sold on the idea that the publisher is not required to render an accounting, officially permitted, or otherwise, qualified services. If advice is necessary, legal, financial, medical or professional, a practiced individual in the profession should be ordered.

This information is not presented by a financial or medical practitioner and is for entertainment, educational and informational purposes only. The content is not intended as a substitute for professional medical advice, diagnosis, or treatment. Always seek the advice of your physician or other qualified health care provider with any questions you may have regarding a medical condition. Never disregard professional medical advice or delay in seeking it because of something you have read.

The information provided herein is stated to be truthful and consistent, in that any liability, in terms of inattention or otherwise, by any usage or abuse of any policies, processes, or directions contained within is the solitary and utter responsibility of the recipient reader. Under no circumstances will any legal responsibility or blame be held against the publisher for any reparation, damages, or monetary loss due to the information herein, either directly or indirectly.

www.ingramcontent.com/pod-product-compliance
Lightning Source LLC
Chambersburg PA
CBHW071226130726
47998CB00002B/846